Alaska

The moon silvers a path across the Talkeetna, the "River of Plenty," one-time gateway to gold fields north of Anchorage. The fiercely grinning face on the preceding page is that of the wolf, a key figure in Alaskan totems.

Alaska

PAUL C. JOHNSON

442865

 KODANSHA INTERNATIONAL LTD.
TOKYO, NEW YORK & SAN FRANCISCO

Drawings by Hirobumi Nagakane

Distributors:
UNITED STATES: *Kodansha International/USA, Ltd., through Harper & Row, Publishers, Inc., 10 East 53rd Street, New York, New York 10022.* SOUTH AMERICA: *Harper & Row, International Department.* CANADA: *Fitzhenry & Whiteside Limited, 150 Lesmill Road, Don Mills, Ontario.* MEXICO AND CENTRAL AMERICA: *HARLA S. A. de C. V., Apartado 30-546, Mexico 4, D. F.* UNITED KINGDOM: *TABS, 7 Maiden Lane, London WC2.* EUROPE: *Boxerbooks Inc., Limmatstrasse 111, 8031 Zurich.* AUSTRALIA AND NEW ZEALAND: *Book Wise (Australia) Pty. Ltd., 104–8 Sussex Street, Sydney.* THAILAND: *Central Department Store Ltd., 306 Silom Road, Bangkok.* HONG KONG AND SINGAPORE: *Books for Asia Ltd., 30 Tat Chee Avenue, Kowloon; 65 Crescent Road, Singapore 15.* THE FAR EAST: *Japan Publications Trading Company, P.O. Box 5030, Tokyo International, Tokyo.*

Published by Kodansha International Ltd., 2-12-21 Otowa, Bunkyo-ku, Tokyo 112 and Kodansha International/USA, Ltd., 10 East 53rd Street, New York, New York 10022 and 44 Montgomery Street, San Francisco, California 94104. Copyright in Japan 1974 by Kodansha International Ltd. All rights reserved. Printed in Japan.
LCC 74-78594
ISBN 0-87011-234-1
JBC 0326-784569-2361

First edition, 1974
Third printing, 1976

Contents

PHOTO CREDITS

Ed Cooper, 37; James Foster, 68–70, 101–5; Velma Harris, 77, 80–84; Paul C. Johnson, 1, 3, 4, 29, 32, 55–56, 63, 88, 93, 106; Scott Kiefer, 33; Robert Levorsen, 51–54, 89, 91, 97; Steve McCutcheon, 57; Einar Nilsson, 72–73; Schallerer's Photo Service, 85, 87, 98–100; Tim Thompson, jacket (back), 15, 17, 19–22, 24–26, 28, 39, 41, 45; Tom Tracy, jacket (front), frontispiece, 2, 5–9, 11–14, 16, 23, 30, 34–36, 38, 46–50, 58–60, 64, 71, 74–76; Howard Weamer, 40, 78–79; Rick Kiefer, 66. All others courtesy of Alaska Division of Tourism.

ACKNOWLEDGMENTS
Of the many individuals who helped with the creation of this book, the author would like to express particular appreciation to the following good Alaskans or Alaska buffs: Commissioner Cameron Edmonson, Alaska Department of Economic Development, Rick Kiefer and Diana Murphy, Alaska Division of Tourism, Juneau; Roger Blair and Jim Johnson, Alaska Airlines; Nick Carney, Alaska Department of Economic Development, Anchorage; Bill Baker and Donna Martin, Ketchikan; Bob Giersdorf, Alaska Tour and Marketing Service, Seattle; and Blueberry John, Nome. Also, a special thank you to the photographers who contributed far more than photographs: Tom Tracy, Tim Thompson, Bob Levorsen and Jim Foster. To all these, a warm thank you.

NOTE: In Alaska there is a custom of writing *Native* when referring to the original inhabitants (Eskimos, Aleuts and Indians) and *native* when referring to other native-born Alaskans. For convenience, this practice is followed in this book.

The Long Thaw

"ONE WORD OF CAUTION to those intending to visit Alaska: If you are old, go by all means; but if you are young, wait. The scenery of Alaska is much grander than anything else of its kind in the world, and it is not well to dull one's capacity for enjoyment by seeing the finest first." So admonished a noted geographer at the turn of the century, and his advice is still pertinent, for few places can match Alaska's variety and grandeur.

The name Alaska comes from an Aleut word, *Alyeska*, which means "The Great Land." It is a fitting name for a country that overwhelms the senses with its profusion of mountains and glaciers, lakes, rivers and inlets, the abundance of its forests and the contrasting barrenness of its frozen wastes. Among the fifty states, Alaska hoards a disproportionate share of blue-ribbon superlatives: the highest mountains; longest day, night, glaciers; deepest fjords, lowest temperatures—and fewest people.

Alaskans delight in pointing out that two Texases could be jigsawed into their state's boundaries. They like to remind visitors that the distance from their state capital to its outermost jurisdiction is greater than the mileage between New York and San Francisco; that their state government rules over an area equivalent to that of West Germany, France, Spain and three-quarters of Italy.

7

Although the state is almost continental in its geographic sweep, it is thinly populated. Half of the state's 320,000 residents live in a single metropolitan area, Anchorage, and three-quarters of the remainder reside in a half dozen cities. The rest are peppered over the state in 250 towns and villages, some with only one or two families.

Thanks to modern technology, these far-flung communities are not too far apart. Bush pilots, endowed with the instincts of birds, serve the remotest settlements, and even the traveler by scheduled airline finds that urban Alaska is no larger than Connecticut or Rhode Island, for he can easily hop around within the state by commercial flights regardless of the season or the weather.

Telecommunications further shrink the state to manageable scale. An Alaskan in Nome presses the touch-tone button for Operator, and the voice that answers comes from Anchorage, 550 air miles away. Beyond the reach of the telephone network, two-way radio connects the most distant village with urban centers of information, enabling a paramedic or a midwife to secure medical advice from a hospital, an Eskimo gambler to place bets on the breakup of the ice in the Tanana River, a geophysicist to check oil data with his headquarters. Special educational television programs are relayed by satellite to tiny settlements above the Arctic Circle.

Alaska today is a yeasty mixture of yesterday and tomorrow. With its rugged terrain, obdurate climate and polar clock, it carries into the twentieth century some of the frontier conditions that long ago vanished in the Lower 48. At the same time, it is rapidly resolving frontier problems with the aid of advanced technology and is swiftly overhauling its sister states.

A friendly people, the Alaskans are cordial and helpful to strangers. One cynical theory holds that they welcome any new face, any connection with the outside world, because the long winters isolate them from their fellows. A simpler explanation suggests that Alaskans have learned to overcome frontier handicaps with cooperation and friendliness. The neighbor in need may be you someday and it pays to be helpful. Staunch individualists, they accept a newcomer for what he is. In their frontier democracy, there is no tolerance for charades, and even the so-called hippie is usually a motivated hard worker. Whatever the rationale, Alaskans welcome the newcomer into their homes, proudly show off their unique land, and proselytize with passionate intensity. The true Alaskan is a walking chamber of commerce.

The first Native Alaskans are presumed to have migrated from Asia. Some evidence suggests that they crossed a land bridge that once connected the two continents. Or they may have sledded across the frozen Bering Strait or paddled their skin boats across in summer. In fact, Eskimo families freely crossed back and forth in this manner until 1926, when the Soviet Union closed the border.

The Native population divides into three major groups: Aleuts, Eskimos and Indians.

Aleuts settled along the chain of islands named for them. Adept seamen, they ranged over the open ocean in one-man kayaks, hunting sea otter and seal and catching salmon. The Eskimos took root along the northern coastline and the mouths of the major rivers. Their culture was based on hunting walrus, seal, polar bear and smaller arctic game. The Indians lived in the interior valleys, where they established small villages or followed the migrating caribou on which they depended for sustenance.

The Natives' encounter with the white man was a cultural disaster of seismic proportions. First to feel the impact were the Aleuts, who absorbed the full thrust of the Russian advance in the 1740s. They fought the invaders but were no match for the Russians' superior firepower and became enslaved.

The Indians along the southeastern Panhandle were next to feel the Russian advance, which they successfully resisted. The Tlingit Indians were brave and resourceful warriors. Well armed with guns acquired through trading and with a limitless backcountry to retreat into, they defeated the Russians and were never subdued.

The Eskimos were barely affected by the Russian incursion. Their major collision with the white man occurred later, when the trading vessels and whalers discovered their existence. Although all the Natives were decimated by white men's diseases, the Eskimos, because of their long isolation, were particularly hard hit. Venereal diseases, measles and, most viciously, tuberculosis carried them off like flies. Those that survived were visited by a later scourge, whiskey, likewise brought by the traders.

Estimates place the Native population in 1740 at the time of the Russian invasion at about seventy-five thousand. This dropped to twenty-seven thousand by 1867. The census now stands at fifty thousand, and though the number is increasing, there is still a long way to go to catch up with the eighteenth century.

Today's descendants are a vital component in present-day Alaska. They largely blend into the general culture. The three groups still keep to themselves; there is little love lost between them—in fact, a bloody war between the Indians and Aleuts was stopped in 1942 by World War II. The Aleuts man the great fishing fleets of the southwest. The Eskimos continue their hunting and fishing and participate with consummate skill in handling complex apparatus involved with the DEW Line and petroleum exploration. The Indians in the Panhandle man the fishing vessels and logging mills.

So wholeheartedly have the Natives adapted to modern ways

that special efforts have had to be invoked to preserve their arts and tribal customs from oblivion. Dedicated dance groups, craft cooperatives and museums are striving to keep alive the rites and ceremonies that the practical-minded Natives long ago abandoned as worn out.

The takeover of Alaska from its long-established occupants began in the 1730s when the czar, Peter the Great, commissioned one of his naval officers, Vitus Bering, to chart the eastern shoreline of Siberia, search for the mythical water route across the polar region to Europe, and learn what he could about the mysterious coast of America.

Bering caravaned supplies over two thousand miles of Siberian wastes, erected a shipyard on the Kamchatka Peninsula, and built several vessels from scratch. In 1734, he sailed one of them, the *St. Gabriel*, north beyond the rim of his known world. He surveyed part of the coastline, discovered the Diomede Islands and the Bering Strait, but he did not sight the coast of America. Encouraged by what he had discovered, he returned to St. Petersburg to request support for further surveys. This was granted, and he returned to his base accompanied by a small army of scientists and observers, including the distinguished biologist, Georg Wilhelm Steller.

Beginning in 1734, Bering dispatched a series of exploring parties. Then in 1741, he launched the fateful expedition that ended his career on a lonely island but changed the course of history. Two vessels set sail, the *St. Paul* and *St. Peter*. They became separated in a storm, and the *St. Paul* continued until it made a landfall at Sitka in the Alaskan Panhandle. This was the first vessel to reach southeastern Alaska. It was not followed until the 1770s when Spanish and English exploring expeditions visited the area. It returned to Kamchatka after losing two ship's boats and several crewmen in an Indian massacre.

Meanwhile, Bering sailed along the Aleutian chain. This was his first contact with the North American continent. Proof that the party had reached the New World was provided in the simple guise of a dead bird: a blue jay. This bird, found on one of the islands was unknown in Asia but had been earlier identified in America. Steller recognized its immediate significance, for it proved to him that they had indeed reached another continent.

Conditions aboard the *St. Peter* deteriorated dangerously. Captain Bering and half the crew were immobilized with scurvy, and there were barely enough hale crewmen on hand to work the sails. A savage storm drove the ship ashore on Bering Island. There Bering died and so did twelve of his afflicted crew. The survivors spent the winter on the island, piecing together a vessel from the wreckage of the *St. Peter*. Somehow, they succeeded and miraculously made their way back to Kamchatka, carrying nine hundred sea otter pelts.

News of the sea otter furs spread rapidly. Vessels of all kinds, even log rafts tied together with rawhide, sailed for the Aleutians. Most of them were never heard from again, but those that returned so enriched their owners that there was no restraining the fur traders. The rush was on.

The shape of Alaska slowly became revealed as the fur fleet scoured the long coastline, slowly working eastward. The trade became so lucrative that it attracted scores of private companies and one-shot operations, which were all consolidated under a government-licensed monopoly, the Russian American Company, patterned after the Hudson's Bay Company.

The Russians gradually exterminated the sea animals as they worked east. Unfortunately, their exploitation of the sea life was matched by their heartless subjugation of the Natives. At first, the Aleuts resisted the intruders, fighting with spears and arrows and massacring ship's crews, but the Russian reprisal was brutal and excessive. Musket and cannon, fire, rape and pillage destroyed the resistance of the Aleuts and they capitulated. The Russians enslaved them to hunt the sea otters in their kayaks; to make sure they met their quotas, they held their wives and children hostage.

By 1800, the Russian penetration had reached southeastern Alaska, where a brisk fur trade was already in existence. The Indians had been trading with British, Spanish and Yankee sea captains since 1790. The Russians decided to break up this trade and moved their headquarters from Kodiak to Sitka in 1802. This shift brought them into the territory of the Tlingits.

Sitka eventually became a lively outpost, a mirror of the life at St. Petersburg. Undisputed ruler of this frontier court was the governor general, Aleksandr Baranov, who held control for nearly thirty years, 1791–1818. A slight figure, addicted to vodka —which he ladled out of a bucket set beside his chair—he was nonetheless a stern disciplinarian, shrewd trader and capable administrator. He supervised a fleet of vessels, a territorial government divided into six districts and hundreds of Russian and Aleut slaves, and turned a handsome annual profit for his company.

In mid century, the hundred-year Russian presence in Alaska began to falter. There had been earlier signs. The sea otter trade had diminished as the animals neared extinction. Demand for the furs had slackened in world markets. As prosperity declined, the large colony became increasingly difficult to feed and supply. Baranov arranged to buy supplies from the Spanish missions in California and even established a branch base north of San Francisco in 1812 to raise produce for Alaska and to further pursue the sea otter. The Fort Ross colony proved a disappointment and was sold in 1841.

The time was fast approaching when the Russians would have to dispose of Alaska. Defeat in the Crimean War in 1856 cooled the expansionist dreams of the court. An agent tried frantically to find a buyer. No European powers were interested but, with great persuasiveness, he convinced the American secretary of state, William H. Seward, to acquire the country at the bargain price of $7,200,000 (the agent pocketed the $200,000 as his commission), or two cents an acre!

By adroit maneuvering, Seward presented the treaty to the Senate in the closing days of the session and, miraculously, steered it to a passing vote. Opposition was minimal, mainly because there was barely a quorum in attendance. When the country awoke to what it had bought, the reaction was prompt, vociferous and angry.

Nevertheless, on October 18, 1867, before a grand military assembly in Sitka, the Russian colors were struck and the Stars and Stripes raised. The United States officially acquired one-half million square miles of territory and a population of 483 whites and 27,500 Natives.

After approving the acquisition of Alaska, Congress took a hard look at the treaty when it came time to appropriate funds to operate the new possession. The legislators were poorly informed about Alaska, and many felt they had been hoodwinked by Secretary Seward. Their outpourings established for the record a host of enduring myths that handicapped Alaska's development for the next century.

Typical of the bombast of the time was the assertion by one representative that "the acquisition of this inhospitable and barren waste will never add a dollar to the wealth of our country or furnish any homes to our people. It is utterly worthless. To suppose that anyone would leave the United States to seek a home in the regions of perpetual snow is simply to suppose such a person insane." Another congressman reported as fact: "Every foot of the soil of Alaska is frozen from five to six feet in depth, and the climate is unfit for the habitation of civilized man."

After a stiff battle in Congress, appropriations to implement the Treaty of Cession were passed in 1868 with just one vote more than the required two-thirds majority. For years afterward, disgruntled legislators referred to Alaska under a variety of uncomplimentary epithets: Icebergia, Walrussia, Polaria, Seward's Polar Bear Garden, Seward's Icebox, and, most enduring, Seward's Folly.

At the beginning, the administration of the new province was entrusted to the army. A company of Indian fighters was dispatched to Sitka on the apparent assumption that the wild land was overrun with murderous redskins. A stoneheaded commander impartially antagonized residents, Natives and Russians alike. Although the treaty granted all the privileges of American citizenship to Russians who chose to remain, they were discriminated against, and within a few months, all but a few of the missionary clergy had left for their homeland.

During the following decades, according to a contemporary account, Alaska was "a country where no man could make a legal will, own a homestead or transfer it, or so much as cut wood for his fire without defying a Congressional prohibition; where polygamy and slavery and the lynching of witches prevailed with no authority to stay or punish criminals."

Bad as conditions were under army rule, they worsened in 1877 when the company was withdrawn to put down a Sioux uprising, and the territory was left completely on its own. What little law and order prevailed was thenceforth generated by spontaneous miners' meetings or vigilante actions. At one point, a Canadian gunboat was called in to quell an Indian uprising because of the indifference of Washington to the pleas of the Alaskans. The navy eventually dispatched a small force to Alaska and later took over the administration of some of the outer islands.

In this dark period, one of the few stabilizing forces was the presence of a scattering of missionaries, who had been sent north by every major denomination to establish churches, schools and medical facilities. One of the most famous of this selfless fraternity was a controversial Presbyterian named Sheldon Jackson, who exerted a profound influence on the development of Alaska. He later became the first commissioner of education when the territory was formed.

The discovery of gold in the 1890s finally began the breakup of Alaska's long isolation. The first findings in 1889 attracted miners to Fairbanks in the interior, but the major stampedes occurred ten years later when gold was discovered in the Canadian Klondike in 1897. In 1899, gold was found in the beach sands at Nome, launching another boom of incredible vitality.

The gold stampede brought the story of Alaska to the front pages of every newspaper. Reporters, magazine writers and scientists flocked to the excitement. Some two hundred camp newspapers blossomed and died in the next decade; many writers launched their literary careers with reports on the new land and its people. Most famous of the literary colony were Jack London, noted for his muscular short stories, and Robert W. Service, the versifier. Among the scientists, the great naturalist John Muir reached a wide audience with his lyrical reports on his glacial explorations of 1870 and 1890.

The evidence of Alaska's mineral wealth dispelled many of the myths about the region's worthlessness, but Alaska's overall development was retarded by a sticky combination of political disinterest and self-interest in Washington, where all authority resided. Alaska seemed light-years away to preoccupied and still poorly informed politicians on the Potomac, who assumed that what wealth might exist was inaccessible because of terrain or climate. The complexities of granting autonomy to "Icebergia" seemed of lesser moment than more pressing problems closer to home.

Once in a while, when pressures mounted to the flash point, Congress tossed a legislative favor to the Alaskans, but such largesse was often negated by the prickly restrictions that accompanied each new concession. In 1906, a representative was admitted to Congress, but he was not permitted to vote. Four years later, Congress made Alaska a district, after rejecting a presidential proposal that the same type of government be established here as had been installed in the Philippines. In 1912, after unremitting pressure, Congress elevated Alaska to a territory.

By contrast, the congressional reluctance to end Alaska's political colonialism was not matched by its enthusiasm for the development of resources that offered immediate sources of income. No restraints on the taking of fur seal, for instance, were invoked until almost the last living seal had been plucked from the Pribilofs, and the only local protection given fishing was a flurry of legislation when foreign vessels started to trespass in Alaskan waters. As mining began to open up the interior, Congress took an interest in financing the building of railroads to haul out the copper, coal and other minerals. But the projects became ensnared in scandal and intrigue, and the first rail line, started in 1902, was not completed until twenty-one years later. Steamship lines, which dominated the transportation scene, flourished under a government-approved monopoly, which squeezed every available cent out of the hapless Alaskan businessmen through exorbitant freight tariffs. The abuses became so notorious that Congress finally broke up the monopoly.

Alaskans found themselves caught in the middle of a profound philosophical debate that echoed in Congress for decades. This was the struggle between factions that believed the nation's resources should be exploited for the common good and their opponents who contended that the country's resources were finite and should be conserved for future generations: in short, a struggle between developers and conservationists. This debate is still unresolved. Visitors to Alaska today see bumper stickers reading SIERRA GO HOME—a rude message to the conservationist Sierra Club to stop meddling in the state's internal affairs.

Perhaps Alaska would still be a territory if World War II had not erupted. The war urgently revealed Alaska's strategic military significance and brought about an explosive increase in federal development. The invasion of the Aleutian Islands, the first foreign incursion on mainland soil since the republic's founding, exposed the vulnerability of Alaska to military occupation, and the wartime emergence of airpower as a decisive military weapon revealed Alaska's strategic importance to the air defense of the states down below.

The ending of the war did not automatically convey statehood. The resistance was still deep-seated. In 1913, a representative had complained: "We have owned this colossal chunk of frozen earth for more than fifty years and have only succeeded in thawing out two or three thousand acres." As late as 1940, an opponent could still point out that statehood would solve none of Alaska's problems, because they were all "due to the extreme climate and hazardous living conditions," and, he sagely concluded, "Congress cannot change the climate!"

Finally, after ninety years of agitation, Alaska was admitted as the forty-ninth state on January 3, 1959. Fireworks lit the winter sky over Juneau, celebrants jammed every bar, gunshots broke the Arctic stillness. Dogs howled and wolves joined the patriotic chorus. The state flag—eight golden stars of the Big Dipper on a field of blue—proudly whipped on flagstaffs throughout the new state. Alaska was no longer a political stepchild.

1. A luxury ferry, under rain clouds typical of the Inside Passage, heads north on its two–thousand–mile roundtrip between Seattle and Juneau.

2. Moored to a narrow shelf at the base of the mountains, Ketchikan's fishing fleet waits for an opening in the salmon schedule, the days, and even hours, of which are regulated by the state.

3. "An old street with an even older occupational history," Ketchikan's Creek Street was once a notorious, boisterous red-light district (closed in 1954), but the houses along it have reverted to more prosaic uses.

4. Tumultuous Ketchikan Creek races past modern apartment buildings, business structures, and the handsome library and historical museum (seen at left).   ▷

5–14. Meticulously copied totem poles in Ketchikan tell stories about people, gods and animals. The originals, carved by Tlingit Indians to honor banquets, funerals, whims, have long since rotted away.

15. Loggers, in unsinkable tubs, jockey rafted logs in a millpond on the way to the chippers.

16. Houses standing storklike on pilings reveal the extreme range of the tides at Wrangell.

17. The aging waterfront of Wrangell, third oldest settlement in Alaska, is reflected in a sheltered arm of Wrangell Harbor.

18. Snow lies on the fishing boats tied up during a storm at Petersburg.

19. Part owner of a gill-net boat, a girl rhythmically coils the bulky net.

20. Norwegian Hall dominates the shore of Petersburg, a Norse enclave. ▷

21. A shipboard crane hoists a purse seine. The red net is the side, the black, the bottom.

22. The catch from a fishing boat cascades into the hold of the tender after weighing.

28

23. Seagulls besiege the catch as purse seiners in dinghies close the net.

25. A two-hundred-pound box of small but tasty Petersburg shrimp represents a small part of a good day's haul.

24. Stowaways, such as starfish, often get snagged in the net.

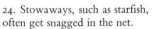

26. Comely lasses of the New Archangel Dance Group in Sitka entertain touring parties with authentic and spirited Russian folk dances.

28. Headstones in Sitka's Russian Orthodox graveyard mark the graves of Indians, who readily adopted this faith.

27. Old Alaskans never die—they simply retire to Sitka's imposing Pioneers Home, which was built in 1915. Smaller state retirement homes are located elsewhere in Alaska.

29. Squeezed between the towering mountains and the water, the booming capital of Juneau clings to a narrow bench along the Gastineau Channel.

30. Auke Lake, within Juneau's city limits, has cabins, fish, a swimming beach, float planes and a grandstand view of Mendenhall Glacier.

31. Juneau's Russian Orthodox church dates from 1894 and became the oldest in southeast Alaska when Sitka's burned down in 1966.

32. Boat owners from all over the Pacific Northwest berth cabin cruisers in Juneau's posh marinas.

33. What fisherman has not longed to be photographed with a forty-eight-pound trophy such as this? Monsters like this keep a host of salmon derbies going each spring.

34–36. Glacier factory in Juneau Ice Fields (*above*): mountain tips rise above compressed snow five thousand feet deep. *Opposite*, an inexorable river of ice grinds its way to the sea. *Right*, the surface is shaped by the bed it travels on. Crevasses form at bends; hummocks reflect uneven terrain beneath.

37. The snout of Mendenhall Glacier dwarfs a hiker. The ice fell as snow, probably two hundred years ago, in the ice field above.

38–40. At Glacier Bay, Muir Glacier is seen dissolving (*above*) and calving (*below*). The blue color of the ice in the cave at left is caused by compression.

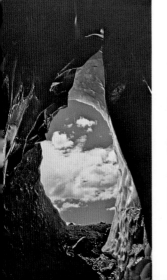

41–42. Nearly forgotten Indian dances are kept alive by the nationally renowned Chilkat Dancers at Haines, while handicrafts on the verge of oblivion are saved by young craftsmen who are taught the old ways by Native artisans.

43. Staging point for the stampede over the mountains to the Klondike in 1898, Skagway basks in its rough-and-ready heritage. Relics from its halcyon days are kept neatly painted and repaired.

44. Transcendentally amazing cancan dancers awake the dead as they revive gold rush frivolity in bistros throughout Alaska and the Yukon. Performances are usually interspersed with recitations of the gutsy verse of Robert W. Service.

Narrow Passages

Although there are three ways to get to the Panhandle (plane, ship or car), by far the largest number of travelers choose to fly or to sail north on a state-owned ferry-liner or cruise ship. The two approaches are as different as night and day.

The big ferry-liner, with a Judgment Day blast of its whistle, glides out of Seattle and heads north for a two-and-a-half-day voyage to the Land of the Last Frontier.

The vessel leaves behind the smoky Canadian lumber ports and hums steadily onward, now threading a path through channels so narrow that the cones on the spruce trees can be seen on either side, now furrowing placid water like a duck on a pond, now rolling through stretches of open ocean. At times, the prospect widens and the eye follows successions of headlands, receding to deep mountain valleys that climb to sharp, snow-capped peaks. Tiny little islets, the tops of submerged mountain peaks crowned with symmetrical stands of spruce, rise above a white ruff of breakers. Mountain and forest, forest and mountain unroll endlessly along both sides as the vessel moves northward.

Signs of life are few. An eagle soars briefly overhead, plummets to the water, and laboriously flies back to its perch with its catch. Gulls swoop and glide in the ferry's turbulence. Occasionally a school of porpoises, arching out of the water, or the

sight of a broaching whale, draws the passengers to the railing.

In this continuous diorama, few evidences of man appear. Toy lighthouses wink on distant islands. Purse seiners slowly circle in the open water. A swift trawler or cabin cruiser overhauls the ferry, its crew saluting the passengers as it hustles past. Once in a great while, fugitive signs of habitation appear: a logging camp, a spindly pier, a lazy spire of smoke rising from a forest.

There is little to divert the traveler's attention from the scenery. No television, no jukebox, no hi-fi. No deck games, no dance floor. No organized frivolity. The younger passengers, who came aboard top-heavy with backpacks and the indispensible guitars, ascend to the top deck, which they quietly take over. Headed for adventure or for a tough round in the logging mills, they rap their way north or wander down to the saloon deck to see how the Establishment is getting along. In the spacious observation lounge, outfitted like the lobby of a first-class hotel, shipboard friendships blossom among the older passengers, and retired couples become instant grandparents as they adopt the children of the young families.

As time wears on, an air of excitement begins to build. The sheer magnitude and extent of the majestic scenery that has filled the horizon for two whole days begins to press upon the consciousness. The forests to port and starboard become more lush, the mountains seem higher, and pinnacles snowier as the destination approaches. The weather closes in. Rain squalls and chill gusts of wind drive the passengers off the deck and back into the snug cabin. Even the sunlight begins to change indefinably. The light is softer, and the sun stays up longer than it rightfully should. With an air of growing anticipation, the first-timer begins to feel that he is approaching a new country, that he has left the United States far behind.

After fifty-four hours at sea, the ferry approaches Alaska's

first port of call, Ketchikan. For half an hour the vessel runs alongside the city, strung out at the base of a mountain range, then with an authoritative blast of the whistle it ties up at the modern dock. A menagerie of vehicles—campers, vans, pickups, sagging station wagons, sports cars—rumbles out like animals leaving the Ark. Then come the passengers, plastic-sheathed against the inevitable drizzle.

The travelers are warmly greeted by a welcoming committee of pretty "Chamberettes," who lure the laggards off the boat and herd the passengers into the center of this picturesque city for a spate of shopping and looking.

This, then, is "Alaska!" (the exclamation point is becoming part of the name here), the Last Frontier, Land of Adventure, Land of the Midnight Sun; home of the Eskimo; habitat of the walrus, polar bear, wolf and caribou; periodic destination for *National Geographic* crews, travel writers, wildlife photographers, hunters and do-gooders.

To arrive by jet is a totally different experience. In place of the leisurely buildup of the long voyage, the jet traveler's Alaska initiation is instantaneous.

The plane leaves the futuristic Seattle-Tacoma airport, quickly ascends above the clouds, and beelines for Juneau. A look out the window provides few clues about the country. A floor of billowy white usually stretches from Seattle to Alaska. Once in a while, a break in the cover permits a stroboscopic peek at a patch of ocean, forest or mountain range. Occasionally, a snow-covered pinnacle rises above the clouds.

After a surprisingly short flight, the plane starts down, sinks into the clouds, down, down, down into gray mist. The first-timer avoids the submarinelike view out the windows and nervously watches the stewardesses for signs of panic. The wheels thud into landing position while there is still nothing but cotton

outside the windows. Finally, after an unsettling interval, the mists clear, revealing a reassuring view of water down below and tiny boats trailing frothy wakes. The stewardesses calmly strap themselves in for the landing. Mountains suddenly appear on both sides of the plane, the jet makes an unnerving, last-second bank, levels out, kisses the runway, and roars into the airport.

The newcomer, somewhat shaken by the theatrical landing, disembarks in a light drizzle. He senses at once that he has indeed reached a new land. Rain forest fences in the airport, snow-capped mountains tower in the near distance, and looming straight ahead rises the massive bulk of a glacier, dirty-white and coldly menacing. A blast of chill air—real or imaginary—greets him. He drinks it all in as he walks through the puddles to the airport building. Exhilarated, he knows that he has indeed left his homeland behind and set foot in a new and dramatic land.

"To the lover of pure wilderness Alaska is one of the most wonderful countries in the world. No excursion that I know of may be made into any other American wilderness where so marvelous an abundance of noble, newborn scenery is so charmingly brought to view as on the trip through the Alexander Archipelago." So wrote the naturalist John Muir of his first encounter in 1870 with the grandeur of southeastern Alaska.

The narrow lacework of islands and peninsulas, generally known as the Panhandle, stretches four hundred miles down the seacoast at the base of the towering Coast Mountains. Over the crest lies Canada.

The densely forested mountains drop precipitously into the sea with only an occasional gap where settlements can be built. Some of the cities cling to narrow benches at the foot of the mountains and stretch out for miles. Juneau, "The Longest City in the World," strings out for forty miles, Ketchikan, for twenty. Skagway is wedged into a compact triangular delta at the outfall

of a river. True wilderness surrounds the cities; half a mile beyond the last street, the untracked forest begins.

Brief patches of highway reach out from the major cities along the shoreline. But they go nowhere in a hurry and dead-end in rain forest. Nevertheless, a surprising volume of traffic hustles up and down the captive roads. Juneau has been compelled to build a freeway from its jet airport to the center of town to accommodate rush-hour traffic. The ratio of car population to miles of usable highway may well be as high as in Los Angeles.

Only at Haines, at the northern tip of the Panhandle, do the roads lead somewhere. Here, a highway links up with the Alaska Highway and the road to Fairbanks. Across the strait, Skagway offers the sole rail connection to the outside world, the narrow-guage White Pass and Yukon Route Railway, which runs to Whitehorse, the capital of Canada's Yukon Territory. Everywhere else, the mountain barricade blocks road development.

Residents who tire of driving up and down the same patch of highway can easily escape by air or water. Hundreds of cabin cruisers, rowboats, scores of float planes, and an efficient ferry system provide ample means for getting around the archipelago. High schoolers think nothing of ferrying or flying five hundred miles to give a concert, stage a play, or compete in sports.

The climate? Mild is the official word for it. Warmed by ocean currents and shielded from ocean gales by offshore islands, the area rarely suffers from extremes of heat or cold. Winter minimums seldom fall below ten degrees, and summer temperatures average in the sixties and seventies. When the thermometer climbs to the upper seventies, natives complain of a heat wave. Snow falls heavily at times, but it rarely remains on the ground except in the higher elevations.

The dominant weather is rain, likely any month of the year but a certainty from October to May. It is a gentle, intermittent drizzle, one stage beyond fog. The amount of the rainfall varies widely according to topography. Juneau records an average of 90 inches a year. With perverse pride, Ketchikan boasts of an annual average of 155 inches—13 feet. The soft downpour barely affects the life-style of the people, who unconcernedly work and play in the drizzle. Sport and commercial fishermen alike ignore it in their quest for salmon, parka-clad hunters stalk game, school children romp on the playgrounds, and steelworkers walk the slippery girders in the rain. But there are many days of glorious sunshine, when the world takes on the exaggerated clarity of a color transparency in the clear, smogless atmosphere.

True, the rain does complicate the endeavors of home gardeners. The natural vegetation grows in such rank abundance that most residents do not feel the need for conventional gardens. But there are many who coax miracles from the waterlogged muskeg and produce colorful displays of hollyhocks, pansies, rhododendrons and azaleas. Some maintain thick, emerald lawns (although swaths of Astroturf are visible in the shopping centers). Local florists do a thriving business selling indoor plants and cut flowers flown in from Portland, Seattle and Hawaii.

As a group, the cities of the Panhandle comprise some of the oldest communities in the state. Some date from Indian tribal communities, some from the years of Russian occupation, and the rest from the 1880s when salmon fishing and logging came into their own. Consequently, the communities are a mixture of venerable and modern. The downtowns are laid out artlessly. Streets wander about like drunken miners. New buildings are tucked into odd-shaped lots wherever there is an opening. Some of the cities have changed little over the decades. John Muir's description of Wrangell as he saw it in 1870 is still largely accurate: "The Wrangell village was a draggle of wooden huts and houses, built in crooked lines, wrangling around the boggy shore of the island for a mile or so in the general form of the letter S, without the slightest subordination to the points of the compass or to building laws of any kind."

These are hard-working communities, which have had little time and less money to beautify themselves for the tourist trade. As a consequence, they wear an air of no-nonsense authenticity, which sets them apart from the look-alike communities in the South 48. Rickety piers, cedar plank sidewalks, maritime cast-offs and rusting junk give a comfortable patina to towns that are acquiring new marinas, seaplane bases, parks and hotels.

The industrious seaport of Ketchikan, "Gateway to Alaska," clings tenaciously to a mountainside that actually comes down to the water at one point, requiring a tunnel to permit the old and new halves of the city to communicate. The turbulent Ketchikan Creek tumbles out of the mountain and boils through the business district, passing apartments, business structures and the striking Centennial Library and Museum. In season, the creek is jammed with salmon rushing upstream to spawn. The creek passes the ghost of roistering Creek Street, a string of tiny houses standing cheek-by-jowl on a forest of piling. It was here that the fishermen came to splurge their season's earnings on women, gambling and hoochinoo, a deadly brew distilled from molasses by the Indians who had been forbidden to buy whiskey and had learned how to make their own. (Yes, this is the origin of the word *hooch*.) This street was a lively spot during Prohibition, when every little house had its secret closet for hiding contraband beverages from the Revenuers.

The city is a busy lumber and fishing port, and its docks are often lined with trawlers and purse seiners, tied up between intervals at sea. Oddly enough, little fresh seafood is served in its restaurants. The catch is rushed to the canneries or the freezing plant or shipped in seagoing tenders to distant processing plants.

On the outskirts of Ketchikan, at the opposite ends of town, stand two of the finest collections of totem poles in the state, assembled in the 1930s by the U.S. Forest Service in an effort to preserve these remarkable works of art from oblivion. Few new ones had been carved since the turn of the century, and, because the lifespan of a totem pole is about seventy-five years at most, it was only a question of time before they would all have disappeared. Even in the 1930s, there were only a third of the poles left that had been counted in 1900.

Totem poles are carved nowhere else in the world and are unique to southeastern Alaska and western British Columbia, where the Tlingit and other Indians developed this highly individualized art form.

Totem poles are story-telling works that summarize myths, legends or actual happenings. The designs are therefore a mixture of realism and fantasy; the characters a mingling of animals, identifiable humans and supernatural creatures. The carvings were often commissioned to commemorate the death of a chief and sometimes contained his ashes in a decorated box fitted into a niche in the base. The work was done by professionals, who crowded the cast of characters into the limited linear space with infinite care and wry inventiveness. They were well paid, sometimes at a rate equivalent to one thousand dollars a pole, and were reimbursed in stacks of blankets.

When a totem pole was finished, it was dedicated with a joyous potlatch, a prolonged festival of dancing, pageantry, feasting and the distribution of gifts. The clans vied with each other in the lavishness of their potlatches, with the knowledge that the guests were obligated to return the favors with equal generosity. Thus, a clan that had given away all its possessions might well get them all back by attending celebrations given by other clans.

At one of the totem parks, Totem Bight, is a reproduction of another long-vanished tribal art form, the community house. Built of adzed cedar logs by Forest Service craftsmen, it is an accurate re-creation of a typical house in which an entire clan lived with its slaves. The house is entered by a single door, only large enough to admit one person at a time and cut low to force an entering party to stoop, thus making it easy to defend.

The sturdy buildings were supported by massive posts, decorated with totemic designs. By custom, slaves were often buried in the post holes at the time construction was begun. The number of slaves per hole was a measure of the wealth of the chief.

The city of Juneau, built at the foot of a pair of mountains that rise thirty-five hundred feet, faces a glassy inlet that separates it from an equally precipitous mountain wall on the opposite side of the fjord. Clouds drift by in low-hanging layers. When the breeze is down, the inlet mirrors the city and its Alpine setting.

Juneau hustles. New government buildings sprout on the hillsides like summer weeds, the result of the transfer of governmental functions from Washington to Alaska following the change from territory to state. The new office buildings, tucked in here and there in the meandering street pattern, rise regardless of weather. Fast-setting concrete and plastic weather shielding permit year-round construction, through rain, snow or sleet.

The city cherishes its past. Tourists are handed maps that show how to find the Governor's Mansion, straight out of *Gone with the Wind*; the charming little onion and carrot Greek Orthodox Chapel; and a favorite institution, the sawdust-floored Red Dog Saloon (1890), which honors its patrons with frameable certificates of attendance. Of a more uplifting nature, the history of the state is stunningly displayed in the Alaska Historical Museum, a modern two-story museum of the first rank.

Juneau was named for the miner who, along with his partner, discovered gold in 1880 in the mountain behind the city. The

Alaska Juneau Mine, unique among mines, operated upside down. Instead of digging down from the top to the gold-bearing quartz, miners bored up from the bottom. An astronomical tonnage of tailings was trammed to the city below, where it was used for building roads, filling canyons and forming breakwaters. The mine shut down in 1941.

Juneau's predecessor as the capital city, Sitka, is likewise proud of its past and makes the most of its long history as the capital of Russian Alaska. During the administration of Aleksandr Baranov, the self-styled "Czar of the Pacific," the Russians operated a frontier version of life in St. Petersburg, with endless partying and intrigues. Though crudely fashioned of yellow-stained cedar logs, the community possessed a number of amenities that astonished visitors to such a remote outpost. Within the stockade were a twelve-hundred-volume library, a museum, an observatory, a forty-bed hospital, and schools where boys were trained in accounting, mechanics and navigation. Three doctors and eleven apothecaries served the settlement.

On top of the highest hill stood Baranov's "Castle," a two-story log structure stocked with "ornaments and furniture in profusion of masterly workmanship and costly price, and many pictures of remarkable merit." In its tower, a beacon burned for a century, the only lighthouse on the island. The remarkable structure burned down in the 1930s.

The present city is located on the site of the third capital. The second was established nearby in 1799 when the Russian American Company moved here from Kodiak to break up the lucrative trade developing between the Tlingit Indians and British, Spanish and Yankee fur traders.

Baranov bartered with the Indians for a site and built a log stockade for the 30 Russians and 350 Aleuts who had accompanied him. The colony remained here until 1804 when the

Tlingits attacked it while the governor and the Aleuts were away and massacred the small garrison and carried off the women and children. When Baranov returned, he found the Tlingits well entrenched in a fortified position, and he was unable to dislodge them with ten days of cannonading. Baranov ordered the building of a new capital on a more defensible site and named it New Archangel. The first capital had been named for Archangel Gabriel, but since the saint had been unable to protect the colony from slaughter, the new site was dedicated to a different archangel, St. Michael. The Indian name Sitka was too firmly established, however, and the Russians themselves adopted it in time.

The Russians occupied Sitka until the American takeover in 1867. Thereafter, the city served as headquarters for the army administrators until their withdrawal ten years later. From then on, it was a capital in name only. There was no police force, the courts were in far-off Washington and Oregon, and the highest ranking official was the collector of customs. The capital was shifted to Juneau in 1900 as part of a governmental reorganization and physically transferred there in 1906.

Present-day Sitka, a charmingly situated city, dwells mostly on its Russian past. Old Russian buildings that escaped a disastrous fire in 1966 are plainly labeled; many of them can be identified on the weathered old maps saved from Russian days. St. Michael's Cathedral, rebuilt after the fire, glows inside with gold leaf, jeweled ikons, and somber-colored stained glass. A fine museum, with a great decorated canoe outside, contains exhibits of Native and Russian artifacts.

Some of the old festivities are preserved. A troupe performs Russian folk dances for tourists. The Gregorian calendar is observed for some of the town's religious holidays, and every year on Cession Day, the Czarist Double-Eagle is run up the flagpole and the transfer ceremony re-enacted.

Totally different from the other Panhandle cities, the noisy railroad port of Skagway capitalizes on its historic days as the entry port for the Klondike stampede of 1898. Gold rush buildings are carefully preserved as reminders of the feverish years when some sixty thousand prospectors disembarked here and started up the long hard trail over the mountains to the Canadian Yukon.

Two dreaded passes led east from Skagway: White Pass (later followed by the railroad) and the more famous Chilkoot Pass, which was steeper but shorter and was chosen by most of the gold seekers. In a grueling saga of grit and greed, the prospectors shouldered their one-hundred-pound packs and slogged single file in a procession that stretched for miles. Men who lost their place in line had to fight to get back in the parade. Hundreds died on the trail. The fearful winter climax was the final quarter mile to the summit, where the icy trail slanted forty-five degrees, as steep as a roof. Once over the top, the men faced further trials to reach Dawson, 460 miles beyond. They slipped and slid down the eastern slope of the mountains to Lake Bennett, where they bought boats or built crude crafts. They rocketed through the Whitehorse Rapids and then floated down the Yukon River to Dawson. Although most of the lurid accounts of this stampede have concentrated on trailside crime, suffering and death, the real story is the fact that thousands overcame the obstacles and quietly mined millions of dollars in gold in the Klondike.

The terrible trail was replaced in 1900 by the narrow-gauge White Pass and Yukon Route Railway, carved out of the mountainsides in an accomplishment every bit as astonishing as the great footsore migration over the pass. Still running today, it hauls freight, tourists and flatcar loads of automobiles to Whitehorse in one of the most breathtaking train trips in the West.

Southern and southeastern Alaska is glacier country. Because of the damp climate more active glaciers are concentrated in the mountain ranges here than in any other part of the state. In the 1870s, John Muir counted more than a hundred small glaciers on a trip up the Stikeen River east of Wrangell.

Some of the glaciers are easily accessible. The Mendenhall outside of Juneau can be visited in a family car, but the most awesome assembly is clustered around Glacier Bay, reachable only by excursion vessel. Twenty major ice rivers flow into the bay, including the great glacier discovered in 1870 by John Muir and named for him. Muir was stirred by the thunderous breakup of the glaciers and described chunks as tall as ten-story buildings breaking off, sliding into the water, and then falling forward with a roar that could be heard for four miles. While he watched, the glaciers calved intermittently without letup. What he was witnessing was the glacial retreat that has been going on ever since, due to a warming cycle in world climate. The snout of Muir Glacier, one of the most active glaciers in the state, is now twenty-eight miles away from the spot where Muir observed it a century ago. Even Mendenhall Glacier has retreated one-quarter mile since 1940.

Visitors to the glaciers are entranced by the eerie blue tint in the crevices in the ice. This coloring is the result of the immense pressure under which the ice was formed. Denser than seasonal winter ice, it is so compressed that its molecular composition is affected, and only the short blue rays of the spectrum can penetrate it. In the late 1800s, ice companies harvested glacial ice here and shipped it to San Francisco, Hawaii and the Orient. As recently as 1972, a group of Japanese businessmen requested an air-shipment of glacier ice for a banquet in Tokyo. Topers in Alaska like to serve it in highballs on the assumption that the dense chunks take longer to dissolve than conventional ice cubes. (They do, but not significantly longer.)

The Booming Coast

A newcomer flying into Anchorage at night may well be astonished by the ocean of lights twinkling down below. Could this be Los Angeles? For that matter, his daytime initiation can be almost as overwhelming. The jet wings across a mountainous wilderness of a hundred Yosemites, austere and lifeless, and then unexpectedly comes upon an immense valley, filled to the horizon with a metropolitan plaid of buildings and streets. What the air traveler looks down upon is half the population of Alaska, concentrated in this booming area.

There are many reasons for this density but the principal one is the temperate climate. Protected by offshore islands, warmed by ocean currents, and shielded from arctic blizzards by mountain ranges, the Anchorage area basks in a moderate climate that is comparable to some parts of California. The annual precipitation is modest, but three-fourths of Anchorage's moisture falls as snow.

The long summer days of the north reach down into Anchorage, where the sun sinks below the horizon for only a few hours during June, July and August. On June 21, the longest day of the year, the sun sets at 9:42 P.M. The extended day affects the internal clocks of all living things, but wild animals, plants and people adjust to it. Alaskans work and play longer hours and sleep less in summer than in winter and seemingly compress a year's activity into the months of summer sun. Plants luxuriate in the extended day. Cultivated crops, though grown within a short season, compress nearly double the growing time into the summer.

The long winter night restores the balance. Life slows down perceptibly, perhaps to make up for the lavish expenditure of energy during the exhilarating months of sunlight. On the shortest day of the year (December 21) at Anchorage, the sun rises at 9:14 A.M. and sets six and a half hours later at 2:42 in the afternoon. People live by the clock but take it all in stride.

Anchorage, the commercial heart of the state, spreads over seventeen square miles. Some 150,000 people live here and in the extended area, and most of them have moved here since World War II. At the start of the war, the population was a modest 4,250. If this growth rate continues, city planners anticipate a population of one-half million within the next fifteen years.

It is unabashedly a typical, modern American city, transplanted intact from the Lower 48. It has less personality than the older Alaskan cities, among which it is a relative newcomer. The oldest building in town dates from 1914 when the settlement, known simply as Ship Creek Landing, was chosen as the supply base for the building of a railroad to Fairbanks.

Though lacking the rough charm of a Juneau or a Sitka, it nevertheless possesses qualities that endear it to its residents. The city is clean, spaciously laid out, and graced with fine residential neighborhoods and a modern downtown. It supports a variety of cultural activities affiliated with the University of Alaska. Once in a while a moose saunters into the outskirts, a reminder that the frontier is still just beyond the last street light.

The city was severely damaged in a destructive earthquake that struck the Gulf Coast on Good Friday in 1964. The 8.6-

magnitude quake (Richter Scale) was the strongest ever recorded in North America and the only major quake in Alaska's two-hundred-year history. The first shock demolished a high-class residential area on a bluff alongside Turnagain Arm in four terrifying minutes. The ground sank thirty feet, collapsing 200 homes and dumping many into the frozen inlet. Downtown, a block-long chunk of a main thoroughfare dropped twenty feet, and stores, warehouses and inadequately built apartments collapsed. A total of 157 business buildings were damaged or destroyed. Miraculously, only 115 lives were lost in the fifty thousand square miles scourged by the quake.

Reconstruction in Anchorage was begun at once and almost all traces of the catastrophe were soon cleaned up. The damaged downtown core was greatly improved in the rebuilding, and the devastated residential area was cleared of the splintered houses and the site left intact as a memorial park. But even here, the tortured ground is healing and in time all the scars will vanish.

Probably Anchorage's main distinction is its role as an air transportation center. The city is a product of the Air Age, and the sky overhead is alive with planes of all sizes, configurations and vintages. The international airport shares with its twin in Fairbanks a volume of traffic that exceeds some of the busiest airports in the Lower 48.

Most significantly, this is the home of hundreds of small planes belonging to the legendary bush pilots, air taxi pilots who will fly anything, anywhere, anytime. More float planes cluster around the hourglass-shaped Hood-Spenard lakes airport than are gathered in any other port in the world. Nearby Merrill Field, another small-plane base, logs more takeoffs and landings than LaGuardia in New York.

If it were not for the small plane and the 6,500 bush pilots who fly them, Alaska might still be back in the Russian era in terms of getting around. Present-day Alaska depends on the plane. One Alaskan out of forty is licensed to fly, an extraordinary proportion, about seven times the national ratio.

Bush pilots have been risking their necks over the Alaskan wilds since the 1920s when the first daring flights were attempted. This swashbuckling fraternity, which originally flew by instinct or a canny reading of terrain, is now assisted by a maze of electronic beacons that guide them safely about. However, some pilots still rely on "seat of the pants" navigation, sometimes with unhappy results. There is reputed to be a small-plane broker in Fairbanks who specializes in marketing float planes abandoned on remote lakes by pilots who landed without realizing that the lakes would be too short for takeoff. The hapless pilots hike out and sell the planes through the broker to anyone who can figure a way to rescue them.

Bush pilots carry passengers, deliver supplies, medicines and mail to remote villages beyond road and river. They pick up hunters, prospectors, skiers, geophysicists and, scariest of passengers, miners who have gone berserk in the long winter night. They fly the injured and sick to hospitals. Many a baby has been born in the cramped cabin of a Piper Cub, including a few of the bush pilots themselves. They fly cows, sheep, racing dogs, bring in mail order brides to lonely miners, and take them back again if they do not live up to the guarantee. One pilot was even requested to rescue a mining community from a curvaceous young siren who was endangering the morals of the settlement.

Not all of them make it back. As the Alaskan saying puts it, "there are old pilots and bold pilots—but no old bold pilots." Some limp home from crash landings with hair-raising tales about repairing crumpled landing gear with rawhide, patching oil leaks with bubble gum, or improvising propeller blades from sled runners and moose glue.

Thanks to the shirt-sleeve summer weather, the most productive farming region in the state thrives in the Anchorage area. This is the famous Matanuska Valley, which produces three-quarters of Alaska's dairy products and field crops.

The long valley is walled by tall, jagged mountains, snow-capped for much of the year and edged with a retreating glacier. Winter is always just around the corner, and the interval between killing frosts is only 120 days. However, the long hours of summer sunshine double the growing season and stimulate the plants to quick maturity but without producing woody or water-logged produce. One well-advertised result of this forced growth is the production of monster vegetables and berries: sixteen-inch zucchini, sweet radishes as big as doorknobs, strawberries that individually fill teacups, peas as large as marbles, and the famous super cabbages too monstrous for one man to carry. Some of these gargantuan creations are raised to win prizes at the state fair held in the valley every year and are not really typical of the average production.

Matanuska made the headlines and the newsreels during the Depression, when it was selected for an experimental work-relief program by the federal government in the 1930s. In a widely publicized effort, the government transplanted two hundred poverty-stricken farming families from the Great Lakes region to Matanuska to launch an experimental farming cooperative. They were chosen from states that had growing conditions similar to those in Matanuska.

The nine hundred-odd people arrived in May, 1935, drew lots for forty-acre plots, and hammered together barns, houses and outbuildings, and cleared the land. One of the first community buildings they constructed was a hospital, completed just in time for a scarlet fever epidemic. It was a busy place in the months ahead, because the newcomers matched the fecundity of their crops and produced a record of 120 babies in the first two years!

The unremitting toil discouraged some of the colonists, some fell hopelessly in debt, some were banished from the colony, and by 1939, 60 percent of the original group had returned to the Lower 48. They were replaced by families selected from a long waiting list, and the colony stabilized at about seven hundred.

Over the years, the valley has struggled to remain solvent. Outside competition has driven out marginal producers and forced the consolidation of small farms into large and more efficient units. The valley is now able to more than hold its own, even though most of its production never gets beyond the dinner tables of Anchorage. The farmers produce excellent potatoes, regarded patriotically as infinitely superior to Idaho's, a large volume of forage crops and marketable quantities of cabbage, carrots, cauliflower, cucumbers, zucchini and turnips. Nearly all of the state's dairy herds are raised here.

Southwest of Anchorage, the forested Kenai Peninsula rises between the open Gulf of Alaska and an inland extension named Cook Inlet, which reaches to Anchorage's back door. The peninsula is a busy petroleum and fishing center and a giant game preserve. Sportsmen flock here by train, car, ferry or float plane to hunt moose, bear, ptarmigan, or to fish for salmon and trout in the numerous lakes, streams, and inlets.

Cook Inlet was named for the British explorer Captain James Cook, who first sailed into it in 1778 in search of the Northwest Passage. He sailed to its end, found his passage blocked, and hopefully tried one of its branches. This one likewise came to a dead end, so, disappointed, he turned around (hence the name Turnagain Arm) and sailed out, ultimately to a brutal death in the Sandwich Islands.

The inlet is at present Alaska's main oil-producing area, and its waters are dotted with ungainly steel platforms. Dozens of offshore wells and an onshore field at Swanson River combine to pump some sixty million barrels of crude oil a year, making Alaska rank eighth among oil-producing states.

Work crews live aboard the steel islands, arriving and departing by boat in summer and by helicopter during the months when the inlet is frozen solid. The tall platforms are specially designed to resist earthquake shocks and are equipped with sophisticated sensing devices to prevent the escape of crude oil into the water. The integrity of the rigs' earthquake resistance was tested in the great quake of 1964, when, though the platforms swayed dizzily, they came through undamaged. The drilling and pumping equipment has thus far leaked very little crude into the gulf, despite buffeting by ice floes several feet thick.

The presence of oil in the waters of the inlet was noticed as early as 1853, when oil slicks were detected off the Swanson River. Exploratory onshore drilling was attempted in 1900 but never pursued. There are still a number of oil seeps in the inlet, and these noxious smelling emanations have been given careful study because of their relevance to the effect on the marine environment of possible leakage from the drilling rigs. According to the oceanographers who have observed them, the gentle seepages establish their own ecological balance. Bacteria break down the oil molecules and the thirty-foot tides flush the emulsification out to sea. Marine plants, fish and crustaceans live in the water with no apparent harm. Experts concede, however, that a blowout from a producing well would unquestionably overwhelm nature's defenses, and the oil companies are taking stringent precautions to avoid such a disaster.

On the opposite side of Cook Inlet, a jagged wall of volcanic peaks fills the horizon. This is the Aleutian Range, a continuation of the necklace of jittery peaks that stretches a thousand miles toward Asia. Some of the volcanoes emit wisps of steam, but most of them are dead craters, rimmed with glaciers that slide down into their cores.

One of the largest of the apparently extinct volcanoes, Mount Katmai, died a spectacular death in 1912. The site of its cataclysmic end is enclosed within a national park (accessible by plane or boat), where visitors can see the stub of the caved-in mountain and the great lava flow that obliterated a forested lake country under one hundred feet of incandescent sand.

The explosion of Mount Novarupta, a few miles to the west, triggered the collapse of Katmai and violent earthshocks and tidal waves along the southern coast. The dust cloud soared into the stratosphere, blotted out the sun for weeks, and lowered temperatures throughout the Northern Hemisphere. Every living plant or animal in the path of the blast was incinerated, and several hundred lives were lost in Native villages within range of the eruption.

Ashes rained down over hundreds of square miles. Kodiak was nearly buried under a three-foot blanket that collapsed roofs and covered ships, rigging, streets and trees. So dense was the cloud of falling ash that the terrified residents could see only a few feet and had to string ropes to guide themselves about the town—or even to the outhouse. Birds, fish and animals perished in the polluted air and water; only the giant Kodiak bears, largest of their species, weathered the catastrophe undiminished, though stripped of their fur by the acid fallout.

The devastated area smoked and rumbled for months afterward and did not cool down enough for observers to enter for three years. A team from the *National Geographic* attempted the first survey in 1915 and was almost driven out. Steam and smoke were still rising from the Valley of Ten Thousand Smokes, the earth's surface was too hot to walk on in some places, let alone bed down on, and all of the water was too polluted to drink.

The scene is deceptively peaceful now. No smokes or geysers fog the air, the rumblings are stilled, and only a wide, windswept vista of desolation meets the eye. The forces that blew up the mountain are muzzled and muffled, rebuilding for another blow some day, hopefully, in some other century.

The ocean side of the Kenai Peninsula presents a prospect of some of the most beautiful Alpine scenery in the state. With fine disdain for the presence of the sea, promoters call the complex of mountains and winding seaways "America's Switzerland." A perambulating ferry system connects the major port cities. En route, the vessel tarries at the Columbia Glacier and jars loose huge ice fragments with playful blasts of its imperious whistle.

Several ice-free ports disgorge a variety of exports—fish and fish products, minerals, shellfish, Native handicrafts—into freighters and tankers, which carry most of the goods to Japan. In return, vessels and barges unload automobiles, mobile homes, beer, ice cream, earthmovers and other construction equipment and Alaskan souvenirs from Taiwan.

All of these ports were severely damaged in the Good Friday earthquake of 1964. The epicenter, in a deep fjord south of Valdez, generated tremendous tidal surges that rushed upon the exposed harbors, demolished docks and warehouses, tossed locomotives about like toys, and carried fishing vessels as far as two miles into the center of town. The ports of Homer, Valdez and Seldovia sank several feet and suffered severe flood damage. Ironically, at Kodiak, two hundred miles to the west, the only seaside structures that withstood the waves and earthshocks were some massive masonry wharves built by the Russians two centuries earlier. The modern wharfage was swept out to sea. All of this widespread devastation has long since been repaired, the fishing vessels replaced, and there is little evidence of the destruction.

The port city of Valdez, so severely damaged by the quake

that it had to be moved five miles to a new site, is now experiencing a glow of long-delayed prosperity. As the southern terminus of the eight-hundred-mile trans-Alaska pipeline, Valdez is in the midst of a prolonged construction boom. Extensive storage, processing and dispensing facilities are being built from scratch to receive the arctic crude oil when it starts flowing in 1977 at 1.2 million barrels a day, more than seven times the present production of the Cook Inlet basin.

The long-range effect of this boom on Valdez has yet to be assessed. Of the thousands of skilled workers needed to build the local facilities, only a handful will be required after the crude is in the line. Fully automated operations will be conducted by a few button pushers and dial watchers. The bulging payrolls of construction days may well be looked back upon with nostalgia.

Valdez got its start in 1898 as an entry port for the Yukon gold stampede. Prospectors chose to disembark here rather than at Panhandle ports because they could hike to the Yukon River over a new trail that skirted the Canadian boundary and avoided inquisitive customs officials. The trail, which led north to the town of Eagle on the Yukon, was laid out by army engineers and was not much easier to traverse than the infamous Chilkoot. The first few miles climbed the steep, icy surface of Valdez Glacier, then entered a high pass, which was often choked with white impenetrable fog; beyond, there stretched 380 miles of wearisome hiking. The cheechakos (greenhorns) arrived in Valdez in poor physical condition, shoddily equipped and shamefully ignorant of the rudiments of placer mining. Most of the misfits were usually weeded out by the first few miles of the trail, but the remainder somehow made it to the Yukon. So popular was the trail that it was soon widened into a wagon road and eventually into a highway. The first 130 miles are part of the present Richardson Highway (named for one of the army engineers), the main north-south artery between the Gulf Coast and the interior.

In addition to shipping and oil, fishing is a dominant commercial activity in the gulf ports. Operating from piers encrusted with netting and brightened with glo-colored floats, fishermen from Homer, Valdez, Cordova, Seward, Whittier and Kodiak account for half of the state's salmon, halibut and herring catch.

Shellfish are the most valuable haul. They are caught by vessels sailing from such ports as Cordova, "The Razor Clam Capital of the World," and Kodiak, "The King Crab Capital of the World." Of the variety of crustaceans netted, the king crab is unquestionably the premium catch. These giant crustaceans, which grow to a six-foot span, can weigh up to thirty pounds. Their delectable meat makes them highly prized. Kodiak honors this aristocrat of crabs with an annual festival and a crab-cleaning sweepstakes.

The beautiful little city of Kodiak, at the westernmost limit of the Gulf Coast, takes pride in its history as the first capital of Russian America from 1792 to 1802. Reminders of the Russian presence are everywhere at hand: an excellent museum housed in a fur warehouse dating from 1793, a fine Orthodox church and an abundance of "sneezable" Russian place-names.

Hunters jet to the island to stalk the formidable Kodiak bear. If Kodiak ever runs out of king crab, it could conceivably promote itself as "The Giant Bear Capital of the World," for the island still has a large population of the largest of all the land carnivores.

45. Crab nets and glo-color locator floats are piled on the dock at Cordova. Alaska's crab capital, its name dates from the discovery of the harbor by Spaniards in 1792.　　　▷

46–48. The M/V *Bartlett* is one of the state ferries that provide lifeline service to roadless communities along the spectacular south central coast. Gaping like an enormous whale, it swallows a load of cars at Whittier (*opposite above*); *above*, it heads into Prince William Sound.

49–50. As a ferryboat gingerly approaches the awesome front of Columbia Glacier, passengers stand by the gunwale to photograph the ice floes. Some of the chunks of ice calved off the head of the glacier are menacing in size. Often the floes are occupied by seals sunning themselves on the chilly pads.

51–54. Noisy confusion reigns during the annual Anchorage Fur Rendezvous; held in late February, it is climaxed by the World Championship Sled Dog Race. Now raised largely for racing, sled dogs are kept in individual kennels.

55. Aerial crossroad between Asia, Europe and North America, the busy international airport at Anchorage is jammed with jets of a dozen airlines.

56. A deckload of trailer homes awaits unloading at an Anchorage dock. Trailer homes are made in the state, but demand still brings them in, often wave battered, from the Lower 48.

74

57. Indicative of Alaskans' dependence on small planes, the world's largest concentration of float planes rings every foot of the shoreline of Hood and Spenard lakes in Anchorage. When the lakes are frozen, skis are bolted on in place of floats, so flying is possible all year round.

58. The milky Matanuska River, laden with rock flour produced by the glacier, winds through the beautiful valley of the same name.

60. Matanuska Glacier, source of the river, keeps company with the Glenn Highway, a direct link to the "Outside."

59 and 61. The well-publicized Matanuska Valley is a major agricultural area. The season is short, but long hours of sunshine and the absence of insect pests make the area productive. Immense cabbages are raised for competition at the Alaska State Fair. In 1973, the grand prize winner received—at one dollar per pound—seventy dollars.

62. The Indian graveyard at Eklutna represents a hybridization of Christian and Native beliefs. After burial according to Greek Orthodox rites, sprightly little houses, containing possessions of the deceased for their use upon return from the dead, are built over the grave.

63. The precipitous slopes of the Alyeska ski bowl offer a choice of runs from "elevator shaft" to "snow bunny." Skiing is possible all year.

64. Captive bergs at the foot of Portage Glacier float only a few feet away from the chilly parking lot. Signs admonish tourists not to climb the delicately balanced chunks of ice, lest they be dumped into the water or clamped in a splitting berg.

65. A sandy plain spreads over a land that in 1912 was transformed from peaceful lake country into a desert; from the river valley, riven by earthquakes, thunderous volcanic convulsions spewed incandescent sand over an area of fifty-three square miles. Now Katmai National Monument, visitors today see only a few wisps of steam.

66. Red pumice covers the slopes of Mount Iliamna, in the volcanic chain that stretches one thousand miles along the Aleutians and runs down the Pacific Coast into Mexico.

67. A waterfall cascades down the mountainside alongside the road to Katmai.

68. Oil from the northern edge of the state will flow through these lengths of pipe stacked at Valdez, the southern terminus of the eight-hundred-mile pipeline.

69. Oil has been pumped for decades from under the waters of Cook Inlet. Crews live and work on these islands of steel, even when the water is choked with ice.

The Golden Interior

The great heartland of Alaska, known simply as the Interior, is an immense mountain-bordered territory that sweeps from the Canadian border almost to the Bering Sea. This spectacular country is a land of rolling plains, part forest, part tundra, accented with isolated mountain peaks and traversed by the powerful Yukon River and its tributaries.

This territory, as large as Washington and Oregon combined, is walled in by two massive mountain ranges. To the north, the Brooks Range stands between the region and the polar lands. To the south, rising between it and the Gulf of Alaska, stands the Alaska Range, capped by Mount McKinley.

Thus shielded from arctic extremes to the north and temperate influences from the south, the Interior combines climatic features from both. Winter temperatures drop to minus 60 degrees and lower, and, by contrast, the summer thermometer often registers as high as 95 above, thus spanning an extraordinary annual range of 155 degrees.

This is the southernmost reach of the nightless day. At Fort Yukon, on June 21 the sun merely rolls along the horizon at midnight and never sinks out of sight. The long night sets in in October and reaches its inkiest climax on December 21. However, it is never completely dark, for the sky carries a faint twilight glow all through the winter months. At Fairbanks, a hundred miles to the south, the shortest day lasts from about 10 in the morning to a quarter of 2 in the afternoon; the longest day stretches from 1 o'clock in the morning to nearly 11 P.M.

The Interior is the grand setting for great nighttime displays of northern lights sweeping and crackling overhead. The cause for this spectacle is gradually becoming revealed as researchers study the phenomenon. Thus far, scientists have discovered a correlation between sunspots and the northern lights, and they can predict when the most dazzling displays are likely to occur following a flurry of sunspots. Research into the phenomenon is highly significant because the displays disrupt radar, aerial flight beams and radio-telephone communications.

The Yukon River is the lifeline of the Interior. Rising in the Canadian mountains, it weaves a braided path through Alaska's midsection, spreads out over an immense delta as large as the state of Connecticut, and empties into the Bering Sea. During the ice-free months, it is a busy thoroughfare, navigable for fifteen hundred miles, as far as Dawson in the Yukon Territory. Barges and shallow draft vessels of all kinds maneuver in its twisting channels, carrying tons of food, building materials, military supplies and produce upstream to the dozens of minor and major settlements along its path. Down come loads of furs, wheat, minerals and petroleum to the freighters anchored offshore. The current is so strong that some small boats that rush downstream after the breakup of the ice never make it back and are abandoned at the end of their journey. In winter, snowmobiles tow loaded sleds up the ice, but the path is a rough one, and the volume of traffic is light.

The thunderous breakup of the winter ice is an unforgettable event. The thick blanket cracks apart with the oar of cannonades, and the broken chunks rush pell-mell downstream, hurried along by the spring meltwater. The flood fans out over the immense delta, filling myriads of potholes and ponds. After the rush has receded, the water remains trapped in the little sinks, as the soil is too soggy to absorb it. The stagnant pools take weeks to evaporate, creating one of the world's finest breeding grounds for mosquitoes.

Typically, thousands of Alaskans bet on the time of the spring breakup. Although wagers are probably placed on every frozen stream in the state, since 1917 the grand sweepstakes has been centered on the breakup of the Tanana River near Fairbanks. A tripod is frozen into the ice and connected by wire to a clock onshore that registers the exact day, hour and minute of the break. Long before the eventful day, Alaskans make their calculations, consulting the stars, numerology and computers, and register their chosen times. Some cautious bettors have been known to cover every minute of their favored day with single bets—at 1,440 minutes in a day, an expensive gamble. Other, more casual gamblers have staked their all on a single dollar and won thousands. The river is capricious, and may break up anytime between April 26 and May 15.

When the ice breaks free, so does Alaska! Thousands of dollars change hands all over the state, and the event is riotously celebrated in every bar, for this is the signal of the end of the long dark night, the end of the quick-freeze cold and the official curtain raiser on spring. The breakup holds the promise of returning sunshine, the rebirth of the wildflowers and the opening of hunting and fishing seasons. The only sour note in this jubilee is the awareness that spring also brings out the famous Alaskan mosquito, jokingly referred to as the "State Bird." Alaskans prepare for the vicious onslaught by stocking up on head nets, ointments, salves, sprays, smudges and even electronic mosquito repellers. The insects swarm from the muskeg and attack any warm-blooded animals within range. Next to man, their taste favors the large ruminants—moose, caribou, reindeer, horses and mules —which cannot escape their torment.

Still largely primitive wild land, the Interior is lightly populated. A large number of small communities are scattered over its river valleys, but there are only a few cities. The unofficial capital, Fairbanks, is a hustling transportation hub and military base town. All forms of transport intersect here: highway, river, rail and air.

Freight barges come up the Yukon, drop off at the Nenana River, and turn into the Chena that snakes through the city. The Alaska Highway officially ends at milepost 1523 in the civic center. During the summer, a steady procession pulls into town: trailer trucks, vans and family cars that have weathered the once-in-a-lifetime drive from Dawson Creek in British Columbia and points south. As an air center, the city is the main freight trans-shipment point for equipment headed for the oil fields in the Arctic. It is also a base for scheduled, charter and bush flights to small towns in the Interior and the Arctic. Fairbanks is the northern terminus of the Alaska Railroad, which runs 450 miles from tidewater, hauling in pipeline equipment, military supplies, food products, mining gear and tourists, and returning south with produce from the Nenana Valley, minerals, timber and tourists.

Like most of the communities in the Interior, Fairbanks started as a gold rush town. A gold strike on the Nenana River in 1902 appeared so promising that gold seekers poured into the area the following spring. The placers played out after a few months, but the settlement remained, and the disappointed miners fanned out in all directions seeking more remunerative pay dirt. They staked out hundreds of claims in the Interior and thoroughly combed it for gold. Most of the sourdoughs left when winter set in, but some gamely worked right through, even though they lacked running water to process their pay dirt. They built bonfires to thaw the frozen ground and dug through the winter, piling their gleanings to one side. When spring arrived, they sluiced their winter's handiwork with water from the reawakened streams.

In their restless wanderings, the prospectors revealed the Interior's richness in minerals; however, they also discovered that successful extraction of the gold would require cumbersome and costly equipment. There being no way to freight heavy gear to the mining areas, the gold fever subsided. It revived briskly in the 1920s after the completion of the Alaska Railroad made it feasible to bring in gold dredges and other heavy mining equipment. The roaring dredges tore their way through the creek beds for a decade before many of them were shut down because of a federal ruling that made their use uneconomical. When the industry shut down, however, the miners had already extracted some two hundred million dollars in gold from the Interior. Furthermore, prospectors had discovered other minerals of equivalent value. Despite the rusting hulks of the dredges scattered about the region today, it is still a producing mining area.

Although Fairbanks was a mining town, it never mushroomed like other boom-bust communities. It grew slowly. By the beginning of World War II, it contained only 3500 citizens and ten years later, 6400. Even now, with the extensive military establishments on its outskirts, it is a comfortable 15,000.

With solid roots that go back three-quarters of a century, the city is an engaging mixture of yesterday and tomorrow. Log cabins, which were still being built in the twenties, huddle against multistory buildings. The city has sequestered the past in an attractive mining village, Alaskaland, composed of houses, stores and mine buildings assembled from here and there. An old sternwheeler chunk-chunks a circuit around a small lake, and another resplendent double-decker takes passengers on a four-hour steamboat ride on the Tanana River. On the outskirts of the city, an immense defunct dredge is kept open for visitors. Off in another direction, a more commercial collection of false-fronts features a few night spots where the dances of the Naughty Nineties are performed to the accompaniment of a tinkly piano. Recitations of "The Shooting of Dan McGrew" and other durable classics by Robert W. Service are given on the hour.

In its own peculiar way, Fairbanks has also added a new dimension to one of the technological burdens of the Lower 48—smog. The volume of vehicular traffic generates a frozen smog that is unique to the area and a baffling nuisance to residents and officials alike. The dense, crystalline miasma collects in low points and lingers on and on, sometimes for weeks. Attempts to dispel it have been unsuccessful, and authorities have threatened to ban automobiles in sections of the city, a Draconian solution that is greeted with anguished howls by the citizens who would rather grope than renounce their vehicles.

Historically, the Interior was slow in opening up. For millennia, it has been the domain of the Athapascan Indians, who settled along its rivers or followed the caribou herds in their grand circular migrations. They hunted, fished, and trapped, and occasionally warred on the Eskimos or Aleuts.

The Indians' viable culture was nearly destroyed by the white man. Russian fur traders and trappers followed the rivers part way into the Interior, working up from the Gulf or in from the Bering Sea. They left little behind, except strings of Russian place names along the river trails and, disastrously for the Indians, some of the white man's diseases, notably tuberculosis.

Americans penetrated the area in 1865, two years before the purchase of Alaska. A survey party for Western Union Corporation received permission from the Russians to survey a route across Alaska for a telegraph line that would cross the Bering Sea by cable and link up with a trans-Siberian wire leading to Europe. This ambitious venture was pursued as an alternative to the just-laid Atlantic cable, which appeared to be a failure. The party mapped a route to the coast and actually started to string wire from the Canadian border when the project was suddenly canceled. The Atlantic cable had begun to operate successfully and the need for the alternative had vanished. However, the party's map, which was the first detailed chart of the Interior, and its report influenced Secretary Seward in his purchase of Alaska.

Telegraphic connection with the mainland had to wait forty-six years before a military line finally brought instantaneous communication to Alaska. The line was completed in 1901-3 by signal corpsmen under the command of an audacious young first lieutenant named Billy Mitchell. In driving the line through from Eagle City in the Klondike to St. Michael on the Bering Sea, he employed a novel strategy. His crewmen hauled in the wire, glass insulators and posts during the winter when horses could pull heavy sleds on the snow. Then, during the summer, the crews retraced the route and installed the poles and strung the wire. He was aware of the historic importance of his mission, and he wrote of the final splicing of the line: "Then from St. Michael and Nome, clear through to New York and Washington, the electric current transmitted our message with the speed of light. Alaska was at last open to civilization."

History of another kind was also being made in 1903 when an attempt was made to climb Mount McKinley.

Plainly visible from Fairbanks 150 miles away, the majestic bulk of Mount McKinley rises above the Alaska Range to the south. The great massif has always excited the imagination of all who have seen it. The Indians called it "The Great One," and, coincidentally, so did the Russians when they came upon it in

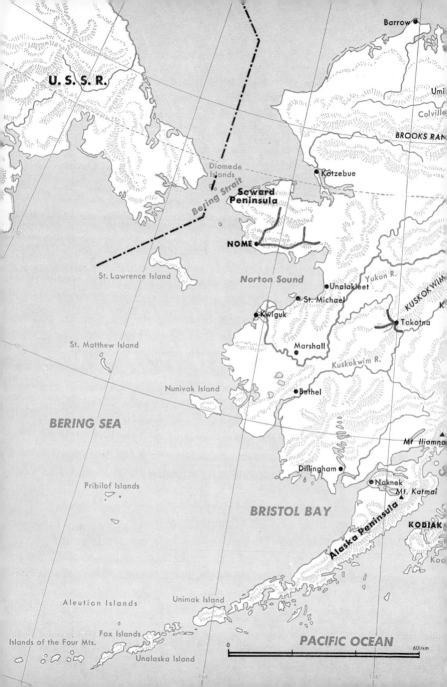

the 1800s. Cook and Vancouver noted the mountain in their journals in the late 1700s. The present name was bestowed by a prospector in 1896. He first called it Denali, a poetic Indian word meaning "Home of the Sun," and then changed his mind and named it for William McKinley because he approved of his monetary policies. Many Alaskans still refer to it as Denali.

The mountain towers above its companion peaks, rising to an elevation of 20,320 feet, not only a record height in North America but internationally unique in terms of vertical measurement. For, unlike most high peaks in the Himalayas and the Alps, which actually rise above valleys already ten to fifteen thousand feet above sea-level, McKinley's base is a mere twenty-five hundred feet in elevation and the ascent to the summit is a sheer three and one-half vertical miles!

McKinley has been an irresistible challenge to mountain climbers since the first unsuccessful attempt in 1903. It was conquered finally in 1910 and has since been scaled by more than six hundred mountaineers. As a technical climb, the ascent of its snow- and ice-encrusted flanks is relatively simple. In fact, the first ascent was made by men without previous climbing experience, who made it to the top of the south summit and back without relying on special clothing, food or equipment. The chief problem is organizing the climbing expedition and transporting the bulky gear to the mountain, a ten-to-twelve-day hike beyond the nearest roadhead. Typically, for example, a party of six that climbed the peak in 1972 spent four months planning the venture, two weeks sorting, packaging and preparing the half ton of food and equipment needed, and forty-four days approaching and climbing the peak and returning to their starting point.

The final climb up McKinley, once a party reaches its base, is an arduous walk up ascending snowfields. The climb is not without peril; crevasses, avalanches, accidents and savage storms that materialize without warning make the climb a risky one, and several lives have been lost to these hazards.

Some mountaineers contend that the ascent of McKinley, like that of other ice-capped peaks in the area, is not as difficult or dangerous as the ascent of some of the lower peaks that crest below the ten-thousand-foot mark. These summits are ice-free in summer, and their exposed rock offers challenges for the most skilled alpinists. The rock is crumbly scree that will not retain climbers' hardware; ice cornices are old and rotten and will not support a climber's weight. Much of the ascent is finger and toe work that would chill the heart of any but the most unflappable mountaineer.

Climbing Denali is just one attraction that draws hundreds of travelers to Mount McKinley National Park. For many, the trip offers an unparalleled opportunity to observe wildlife. The park was created in 1917 as a game preserve, to protect the wild animals from the hordes of hunters that were expected to rush to the Interior when the Alaska Railroad was completed.

The park is a veritable open-air zoo, where observant visitors can see wildlife going about their daily chores. Most of the animals are shy, however, and many travelers choose to take the guided wild animal tours sponsored by the park service. The tours leave the headquarters area at the unholy hour of 4 A.M., the hour when the animals are up and about.

Ungainly moose are often seen ambling about the meadows or browsing in reedy ponds. Generally amiable animals, moose are noted for disputing the right-of-way with motorists and train engineers, who gallantly give way. Grizzlies and black bears are occasionally seen, fishing in the streams or foraging for berries. At one point along the access highway, grizzlies are so plentiful that motorists are forbidden to stop.

Smaller animals abound. Dall sheep inhabit the slippery scree along the mountainsides, relatively secure from their natural predators because of the uncertain footing that they alone can negotiate. Red foxes are plentiful, and so are the staples of their diet: snowshoe hares, parka squirrels, lemmings and nesting ptarmigans. Wolves roam the park but are rarely seen. Their presence is revealed at night by their spine-tingling calls.

By far the most dramatic animal pageant in the park is the annual migration of the caribou in late June. Herds numbering as many as five thousand animals slowly graze their way through the park on their way to summer range in the Arctic.

The Frosty Arctic

Arctic Alaska encompasses all the extremes that many people once attributed to all of Alaska—frozen ground, absence of trees, quick-freeze cold, the endless night—and yet it is one of the most thoroughly fascinating areas in the state. Travelers are beginning to "discover" the Arctic as a rewarding destination, winter or summer, thanks to the energetic promotion of airline companies.

The Arctic runs along the northern and northwestern edge of the state, much of it wedged between the Brooks Range and the Arctic Ocean. Frozen over for eight months of the year, the region is encased in a sheath of ice that runs right out into the sea, wedding land and water in a continuous icy sheet. As might be expected, temperatures remain low throughout the winter, hovering around twenty degrees below zero, but, paradoxically, they are not as low as those in the Interior, probably because of the tempering presence of the sea. The ice cap melts away in the spring, under the unblinking sun, and summer temperatures rise into the sixties and seventies. Offshore, the ice cracks up and melts, permitting the safe passage of oceangoing vessels.

Much of the Arctic receives very little precipitation (no more, in fact, than Phoenix, Arizona), but the little that falls as snow remains, permanently frozen in the ground. The permafrost may be only a few feet deep in some places; in others, it goes down two thousand feet. It is covered with a treeless mat known as tundra, a foot-deep layer of mosses, sedges and dwarf forms of trees familiar in the Lower 48, such as willow, dogwood and spruce. When the spring thaw arrives, the plants hurry into blossom, compressing their life cycle into the four months of sunshine. A bright carpet of wildflowers flares into bloom, some as tiny as collar buttons, produce seeds, and die down for the frozen sleep.

The surface looks like a soft and inviting carpet for walking, but let John Muir describe the sensation when he tested it in 1881: "The barren lands of boggy tussocks promise fine walking, but prove about as tedious and exhausting as possible. The spongey covering is roughened with tussocks of grass and sedge, creeping heathworst and willows, among which the foot staggers about and sinks and squints, seeking rest and finding none, until far down between the rocking tussocks."

Life on the tundra throbs with the miracle of renewal during the weeks in the sun. Even before the ice is completely melted, sky-darkening flights of birds arrive from the south, heading for their nesting grounds. They peck through the ice for last season's crop of flowers and seeds, impatient for the new growth. The air vibrates with their songs, accompanied by the humming of insects and the surly drone of mosquitoes.

By October, the game is up. Ice floes start forming offshore and the rivers start to freeze. The moose retire to forested areas to wait out the cold, caribou swing south, bears den up, and the lemmings burrow underneath the forming ice, content to spend the winter actively foraging under the ice blanket. Foxes, hares and ptarmigan exchange their summer camouflage for snowy white. All the migratory birds, their flocks swollen by the summer young, head south. Only the snowy owl and the raven remain.

The tundra is a fragile plant community, living in a thin blanket of soil on top of the permanently frozen earth. It is easily damaged and its scars heal slowly, if at all. Footprints may become a permanent part of the landscape, and the tracks of vehicles can become gullies, erosive streams, wherever the insulating surface blanket has been removed to expose the permafrost to the sun's warmth.

The low-growing plants are the dietary mainstay of the caribou that migrate here for the summer. Accompanying the herds are small but deadly convoys of wolves that skillfully cut out the old, ailing and very young. These predators, the last of their species in the United States, hunt as a team. They live model communal lives within a strictly structured society that dictates the duties of every member of the pack.

The wolves' ecological role is a matter of acrimonious debate in Alaska. The wolf has two-legged enemies who contend that it should be hunted like any other game animal. Although the wolf is furtive, and difficult to trap or poison, it is vulnerable to airborne hunters, and many pelts have been taken in this manner. In defense of the wolf, a number of biologists contend that the animal is a necessary fraction in the Arctic food chain. Their depredations keep the number of caribou in check, and their preference for the weak and maimed keep the herds healthy.

Another member of the deer family, the reindeer, is probably better known outside of Alaska because of its key role at Christmas. These animals were imported from Siberia in the 1800s and are raised like cattle. The Eskimos use dogs and snowmobiles, which work as well on tundra as on snow, to herd the wild, skittish and unpredictable animals. Reindeer are raised as a meat supply—steaks taste like beef—and for their hides. Herds are sometimes seen by tourists in the Nome area.

Perhaps the most puzzling of the Arctic mammals is the soft-ball-size lemming, a burrowing animal noted for its fecundity. It serves as the main course for a host of predators. For reasons not yet understood, lemmings go through seasons of prodigious reproduction, and the predator population zooms. At other times the fuzzy little animals go into periods of sharp decline, and the dependent predators, desperate for food, shift to other game or starve. One thing the Alaska lemmings do not do is to commit mass suicide. This well-publicized custom may be followed by some of its European cousins, but the only time they drown in Alaska is when hordes attempt to cross a rushing river.

The tundra and the frozen periphery of Alaska have been the home of the Eskimos for centuries; a resourceful people, they have perfected a viable culture under the most trying conditions. Over the generations, they have developed effective ways of encapsulating themselves from the cold with warm, waterproof, insulated clothing and snug shelters. (But not igloos! These snow houses were never built in Alaska.) Hunters to a man, they derived all the necessities from game: food, clothing, heat, light, medication, tools, weapons and ivory for art objects. They made their boats from the skins of walrus sewn over driftwood frames, their tents from skins laced to driftwood poles. In summer, the men hunted walrus, seal, and in their skin cockleshells valorously pursued whales. In winter, they searched the ice floes for seals, occasionally killed a polar bear. In summer, they caught salmon, which they filleted and dried in the sun and wind.

Their compact with nature was a fragile one, however, and sometimes nature won. John Muir wrote about visiting a village in 1881 "where every soul of the population had died two years ago. More than two hundred skeletons were seen lying about like rubbish; in one hut, thirty, most of them in bed."

A happy people—perhaps because of the self-confidence engendered by their conquest of a harsh environment—they are family oriented, with strongly differentiated roles for man, wife, children and relatives. They treasure their children, who represent their stake in the future. There is little tolerance in their society for the weak and the ailing, for their survival depends on the combined labor of all. Modern living conditions have relaxed this standard considerably, but at one time, in periods of famine they set girl babies and aging grandmothers out in the snow to die.

The Eskimos are master craftsmen, skilled in building, trapsetting, sewing, repairing. Their survival often depended on the workmanship put into mukluks (the world's best boot), waterproof raingear (strips of walrus gut sewed together with waterproof stitching), or the integrity of parkas, pants, mittens that could result in death if breached in the quick-freeze cold.

Evidence of the Eskimos' dexterity and artistic talents is everywhere on view in gift shops throughout Alaska. With meticulous detail, Native craftsmen recreate their daily lives in miniature, carving from walrus tusks or mastodon teeth. At their best, these exquisite works are of museum quality, and museum prices, too. The shops are also flooded with casual works, perhaps whipped off in an hour or so to exchange for a drink or some pocket cash, which are used for cigarette lighters, cribbage boards, letter openers, toothpicks, earrings, cuff links. Wellcrafted gold jewelry, jade carvings, leather work, mittens, parkas, boots and dolls also fill the shelves in many shops.

Like the other Alaskan Natives, the Eskimos suffered in their contact with the blessings of the white man. Diseases introduced by traders and whalers decimated the population. Along with the epidemics came whiskey, a pernicious introduction. With no racial experience with alcohol, some of the Eskimos came to depend on it to relieve the tedium of the endless night. The combination of hoochinoo and the dark night, aggravated by the monsters that peopled their superstitions, was too much for some, and all too many of them went insane.

With commendable zeal, missionaries sledded hundreds of miles to rescue the Eskimos from themselves and to bring them the benefits of Christianity. They disapproved of some of the Eskimos' quaint customs (wife sharing, for instance) and their dark superstitions and set about educating them in the ways of righteous living and instructing them in the *ABC*s. They converted many to their faith, instilled the seeds of learning, and introduced medical care for the first time in many villages.

Eskimos today are in transition, caught between their old ways and the beguiling and less burdensome life that they see around them. For some, adoption of Western ways is too dislocating, and many have suffered mental breakdowns or retreated into alcoholism. Even those who have adapted have had to make radical adjustments in their life-style, principally since World War II. Their children are receiving advanced education in Alaska's excellent school system and are sent out to Indian schools in New Mexico. Adults are employed in the expanding bureaucracy, oil companies and air transport. Their dexterity makes them adept mechanics and technicians, and hundreds are employed for the first time in high-paying jobs. Their new prosperity is spent on improved housing, better clothing, a more varied diet, work-saving appliances and, significantly, outboard motors and snow-mobiles.

The snowmobile symbolizes the transitional status of the Eskimo because it marks a radical change from a barter to a cash economy. The dog team was once the sole means of overland transportation within the Arctic. The teams were more or less self-supporting. The sled, its hardware and the dogs' harness were all fashioned from materials close at hand. On a trapline, the dogs were fed the carcasses of the animals caught in the traps.

Even when not working, they lived on dried salmon, a food that cost nothing but effort on the owner's part. The furs picked up with the help of the dogs could be swapped for food, hardware or even some cash.

By contrast, the snowmobile stands outside the barter chain. It must be paid for in hard cash, distributed over easy payments, to be sure, but requiring steady employment on the part of the purchaser. Repairs and gasoline likewise cost money. Nevertheless, the snowmobile has caught on and has nearly swept the dog sled into oblivion. The machines are swift and exciting to drive, easy to use, require no food when idle, and convey prestige as they roar through the village.

But the old dog team dies hard. Its obituary was written in the thirties when newspapermen dourly predicted that the bush plane would make the dog sled obsolete. It did not. Similar predictions are now being made about the snowmobile versus the dog sled. Time will tell. In the meantime, the art of dog sledding is being vigorously kept alive in the dog-racing world.

Partisans of the sled dog write off the snowmobile. A romantic glow surrounds the legend of the dog team. Writers since Jack London have described the mystical relationship between a musher and his team. Descriptions written today portray the team leaders as smarter-than-human animals that make Lassie look like a stupid mutt. A sharp leader, usually a bitch, possesses noble virtues: ability to lead the pack, subdue recalcitrance, defend the team against outlaw dogs, and, most important, follow a trail with unerring instinct. A good leader that has been over a trail once can find her way back with no trouble. Many a team has been led safely and surely through blinding blizzards and white-outs by the canny instinct of the leader, while the superfluous human in theoretical command hangs onto the sled, blind, lost, and trusting. Unlike a snowmobile, if a team is involved in a mishap that sets them free, they will race home, enabling the villagers to retrace the trail and find the stranded musher.

Village councils respect the difference. They permit a lone trapper to set out on the trail with his team but they forbid solo snowmobiling. At least two machines must go out together. A breakdown fifty miles from camp in a snowmobile can be a serious, if not fatal, occurrence.

Dog team racing received its biggest boost through the initiation of the one-thousand-mile Nome to Anchorage race known as the Iditarod. This grueling contest takes about three weeks to complete, but the large prizes are well worth the effort. Rules require that the contestant must finish with the same number of dogs as he started out with. If any die or take sick along the way, he has to carry them "in the basket" on the sled.

The starting point of the Iditarod race, Nome (population twenty-five hundred), is a fascinating town, the self-proclaimed capital of Arctic Alaska, situated on the Seward Peninsula with its back to the Bering Sea.

Nome is deceptively drab in appearance. Standing well north of the timberline it has only one tree, a single specimen of a dubious species that is pointed out to all tourists. The houses and business buildings, many of them unpainted, lean this way and that, reflecting the uneven footing on permafrost. Some are kept level with house jacks; some are mounted on skids so they can be moved to a new lot if the old one turns into a quagmire.

In contrast, a half dozen modern structures—a federal building, library and museum, and two inns—stand foursquare on the only strip of land that is not permafrost. This happens to be the west side of Front Street, the main street, which runs parallel to the shoreline only a hundred feet from Norton Sound, an arm of the Bering Sea. These buildings are protected by a massive stone breakwater completed in 1951 to shield them from the fury of storms. Before its construction, the downtown area was periodically wrecked by rampaging waves. The business district was destroyed in 1913 and was almost ruined as recently as 1946. Local legends tell of boats being driven across Front Street to the tundra behind, of driftwood logs being tossed over the rooftops and of a wind-driven log smashing through the wall of a bar into an occupied rest room. Nomeites tell of a noble bartender who chose to go down with the ship, staying loyally behind the bar as the waves carried his building out to sea.

The city basks in a rambunctious history, for it was here that the final curtain rang down on the gold fever of the turn of the century. Gold was discovered in a nearby creek in the fall of 1898, and word inevitably leaked out. By the following spring, prospectors were headed Nomeward down the Yukon River and up from Seattle by ship, racing to see which group could arrive first. Prospectors swarmed over the hills back of the city with generally unexciting results, but when one of them accidentally discovered that the beach sand between the tides contained panable gold, the last of the great gold stampedes was soon under way. Steamship companies in Seattle shamelessly promoted sailings to Nome, advertising that "The Golden Sands of Nome" stretched for two hundred and fifty miles in a strip twenty-five miles wide—so richly laden that gold clung to ships' anchors.

The truth was far from this radiant picture. The gold-bearing sands were actually confined to a narrow strip three-quarters of a mile long, and this was staked out by the first miners to arrive.

Nevertheless, an incredible surge of humanity poured ashore, and the mess on the beach assumed gargantuan proportions. Tents were pitched twenty deep for three miles. Stacked on the sands were mountains of supplies: barrels of beer and whiskey; bags of beans and flour; acres of lumber (the nearest forest was seventy-five miles away); furniture, pots and pans, bedding, sea chests and trunks; mining gear—pumps, pipe, hose, steam thawers, gold rockers. "As odd a conglomeration as ever eye rested on," reminisced an eyewitness.

Over the months, a total of thirty thousand men and women disembarked here. Though most of them returned home empty-handed, a vigorous mining activity continued for seven or eight years. A respectable-looking downtown metamorphosed, with lodges, churches, innumerable bars and an opera house. The wealthier miners developed a social whirl. Nome's "400" imported costly furniture, rugs, draperies and bric-a-brac. The women sent to Paris for the latest styles, which they wore through the mud and snow. One member of the elite later recalled, "Beneath sweeping trains they wore long woolen underwear to protect themselves from the winter cold. Some of the dresses had plunging necklines and you'd see a touch of red wool showing at the bottom of the V."

Despite this elegance, there were several harsh realities, traceable to the permafrost. Simply stated, there was no plumbing. Drinking water was sold house to house from tank wagons, and sanitary facilities were limited to chemical toilets, known locally as "honey buckets." The only bathtub in town was used by its owner to store wet boots, raincoats, and dog harnesses. A bathhouse rented a tub, soap, and towel for forty cents.

As the placers declined, heavy dredging equipment moved in. The task was not easy because of the frozen earth. Steam jets were used to soften the gold-bearing soil until it was discovered that cold water would do just as well. A ditch was dug into the hills for several miles to collect water for the dredges. It can still be seen in back of Nome; in fact, some of the city's water still comes from it. Ultimately, these monsters lost out to economics. The boom ended by 1910, and the destruction of the business district in the storm of 1913 finished it.

Nome today is an engaging blend of tourist trap and hard-working city. Travelers pour in during the summer, but so do carpenters, road builders and a host of craftsmen who rush to spruce the city up for the months of "the white silence." Tourists drop in at the bars, which stay open all night, to sample the Tanglefoot or the Bering Ball, two local concoctions of lethal propensities. They crowd the gift shops, meet sled dogs, pan gold, and, climax of the visit, watch the superb King Island Dancers perform Eskimo dances.

A city of a totally different kind is rising several hundred miles to the northeast at Prudhoe Bay, the northern terminus of the Alaska Pipeline.

Set in the midst of total desolation, it is a product of the black-gold rush. It looks like an enclave out of science fiction. Crews live encapsulated in great movable trailers, comfortably heated, with showers and dining areas. A large community center, with a live tree from Wisconsin growing in its lobby, features swimming pools, saunas and game rooms. Tapes of television programs are flown in for entertainment.

The crews work with huge, brutal machines, specially designed to operate in minus sixty degree weather. Their task is to bring oil from deep below the two thousand feet of permafrost and send it down the four-foot pipe to the Gulf of Alaska.

In winter, equipment was trucked in over the so-called Hickel Highway (named for the former governor of Alaska and secretary of the interior). Immense trucks and trailers safely haul supplies over the frozen tundra, following a route that is gradually being paved for year-round use. More specialized equipment is flown in from Fairbanks in giant cargo planes or carried by immense, implausible-looking helicopters, powerful enough to pick up a large trailer or a complete drilling rig. With the help of flocks of smaller helicopters, prospecting and drilling operations are kept from damaging the tundra. One of the most unbelievable of the aerial armada working here is a small Swiss plane with a nose like an anteater. The turbine-powered craft, which was developed for glacier rescue work in the Alps, can take off and land at twenty miles an hour.

The construction of the pipeline has been a subject of heated controversy. Environmentalists blocked the building of the line for three years because they charged it would destroy the tundra and break up the migration of the caribou by imposing a barricade across their path. There was sufficient validity in their contentions to warrant careful restudy by oil company, government and university engineers. The crude oil flows from the depths of the earth at 140 degrees and would maintain this temperature all the way to Valdez. It was feared that the warmth would melt the permafrost and cause irremediable damage to the tundra. The engineers finally came up with a design that solves both problems. The cost is three times that of the original plan, but it will be worth it in terms of minimizing the impact on Alaska's ecology.

There is still lingering concern over the possibility of a break in the pipe cascading millions of barrels of hot crude oil over the tundra. This nightmarish prospect is also one that the engineers now feel is solved. Hopefully, they are right. At any rate, ready or not, the big pipe will presently be delivering Alaska crude to the oil-thirsty Lower 48.

70. *Opposite*, the wispy aurora borealis flares, sweeps, and dances in a perpetual light show in the winter skies. Northern lights occur all through the year but are most visible during the long night.
▷

71. *Overleaf*, the highest peak in North America, snow-mantled Mount McKinley rises 20,320 feet above sea level.

72–73. Members of a U.S. Army team, testing cold-weather gear on Mount McKinley in 1947, confront a formidable obstacle near the summit and pause to reconnoiter. *Below*, an army mountaineer studies a slender ice bridge before venturing to cross.

74–75. Alaskan pilots will land anywhere, including Mount McKinley. Having brought his ski-equipped plane down on a smooth stretch of glacier, a bold airman calmly pitches camp.

76. So vast is Mount McKinley that it is almost a mountain system in itself. The glaciers that originate on its summits and plough down its sides include the majestic McKinley Glacier, here viewed from a bush plane.

78. After the brief Arctic summer, the sweeping tundra, which stretches to the polar seas, takes on the somber colors of autumn.

79. Harbinger of spring, moss campion breaks through the ice, impatient for its turn in the sun.

77. A lordly bull caribou surveys his domain. Munching on low plants, caribou meander north in herds of ◁thousands.

80–81. A drenched brown grizzly waits in the rapids to snatch a salmon from the torrent. The red fox hunts rodents, snakes and, sometimes, plump ptarmigans.

82–84. Moose favor boggy areas, where they graze off the bottom of standing pools as easily as on dry land. *Below left* is a male ptarmigan, partly winterized, and *below right* an elegant waterbird, the loon, often found in association with moose.

85. Forcing a passage upstream to spawn, salmon are tossed into the air by their violent maneuvers. Their way is beset by a gauntlet of predators, human and animal.

86. An ingenious fish wheel, when revolved by the current, lazily scoops fish out of the river and dumps them into a box on one side.

87. Trappers' caches, a common sight in wooded areas, are used to store food and pelts beyond the reach of marauding animals.

88. Spring sunset, 11:30 P.M.: couples clamber over the breakwater along the frozen, pastel-hued Bering Sea at Nome. ▷

89–90. A masked dancer strikes a forceful pose as he performs a story-telling dance. Drummers, beating on drums made of walrus stomach and driftwood, chant the story in rhythmic chorus. Nome's King Island Dancers are one of the best-known troupes preserving Eskimo dance traditions.

91. An Eskimo craftsman scribes walrus ivory with the bow drill that has been used for generations. The butt end rests in a mouthpiece, the drill point is directed by one hand, and rotation is supplied by whipping a bowstring back and forth.

92. A bone breaker for the uninitiated, the blanket toss is mastered in childhood by Eskimos. Now a casual sport, it is thought to have originated as a hunter's maneuver to spy for game. The best revolving lookout could scan the entire horizon.

93. A staunch umiak rests on its winter rack. Sewn walrus hides over a driftwood frame, these boats have served Eskimos for millennia. The newest ones have a transom for an outboard motor.

94. Most Eskimo villages are located on water within easy range of the seal bounty. Store-bought skiffs with outboards are being adopted in place of oar-propelled skin boats.

95. Winter bears down hard on shoreline Eskimo villages but no longer seals them off completely. Inhabitants come and go by snowmobile, or by bush plane, and in an emergency summon aid by radio.

97. Children are dressed with elaborate care.

96. Strung on racks, strips of ◁ salmon meat dry in the sun.

98. An Eskimo woman smilingly displays a fish caught in the age-old way—through a hole in the ice. Despite the rapid modernization of Eskimo life, the bountiful sea is still the best of supermarkets.

99–100. Camouflaged in white parkas, hunters push through the ice in search of walrus, which can now be taken only by Eskimos and only for sustenance. Divided up among a party, the carcass provides food, clothing, tools, light, heat, medicine and ivory.

101. Geophysicists build an igloo to relieve tedium.

102. Aircraft are an outpost's lifeline: ski planes, helicopters, a plane that lands at twenty miles per hour, and cargo planes like the one below.

103–104. A self-contained town rises at Prudhoe Bay, northern end of the Alaska Pipeline. The dreaded Arctic holds few terrors for the crewmen, who lead encapsulated lives in track-mounted trailers that contain all the amenities of home—except women.

105. Hunters roar off into the mists on snowmobiles, towing sleds with all their gear. Unlike dogs, the machines do not have to be fed when idle.

106. Left behind is the faithful sled dog, such as this proud mother and her litter.

THIS BEAUTIFUL WORLD